WALKING DISTANCE

SO-AZC-135

WALKING DISTANCE

Debra Allbery

University of Pittsburgh Press

Pittsburgh • London

The publication of this book is supported by grants from the National Endowment for the Arts in Washington, D.C., a Federal agency, and the Pennsylvania Council on the Arts.

Published by the University of Pittsburgh Press, Pittsburgh, Pa. 15260
Copyright © 1991, Debra Allbery
All rights reserved
Eurospan, London
Manufactured in the United States of America

Library of Congress Cataloging-in-Publication Data

Allbery, Debra. 1957–
    Walking Distance / Debra Allbery.
      p.   cm. — (Pitt poetry series)
    ISBN 0-8229-3687-9 (cl.). — ISBN 0-8229-5458-3 (pb.)
    I. Title. II. Series.
PS3551.L377W35   1991
811'.54—dc20   91-50111
                                              CIP

A CIP catalogue record for this book is available from the British Library.

Grateful acknowledgment is made to the editors of the following publications, in which versions of these poems first appeared: *Crazyhorse* ("Outings"); *The Iowa Review* ("Produce," "Next-Door Neighbors," "Stone Soup," "Instinct"); *Ironwood* ("Assembler"); *The Kenyon Review* ("Sherwood Anderson Walks Out," "Sentiment"); *The Missouri Review* ("The Reservoir"); *The Nation* ("In the Dream She Doesn't Tell Him"); *Ploughshares* ("Carnies"); *Poetry* ("Offering," "Children's Story," "Walking Below Zero You Tell Yourself," "Forgiveness"); *Poetry Northwest* ("Protection"); *Prairie Schooner* ("Money"); *Soundings East* ("Twelfth Thanksgiving," "Getting Religion," "False Starts"); *Western Humanities Review* ("Background, 1969") and *The Yale Review* ("Tour of Duty").

"Instinct" was reprinted in *The Creative Process: Ten Years at Ragdale* (Ragdale Foundation, 1986).

The epigraph on p. vii is excerpted from "Action," from *Fool for Love and Other Plays* by Sam Shepard. Copyright © 1984 by Sam Shepard. Used by permission of Bantam Books, a division of Bantam Doubleday, Dell Publishing Group, Inc.

I wish to thank the National Endowment for the Arts, the New Hampshire State Countil on the Arts, Phillips Exeter Academy, the DiLisio Foundation, and Chubb LifeAmerica for fellowships which provided time to write these poems, and the MacDowell Colony, Yaddo, Ragdale, and Interlochen Arts Academy, who provided stimulating and supportive environments.

My deepest gratitude also to Paul Bennett, Jane Cooper, Rod Kessler, and Alan Williamson for their encouragement and guidance.

for my parents,
James Allbery
and
Janice Starr Allbery

*Just because we're surrounded by four walls and a roof doesn't
mean anything. It's still dangerous. The chances of something
happening are just as great. Anything could happen. Any move is
possible. I've seen it. You go outside. The world's quiet. White.
Everything resounding. Not the sound of a motor. Not a light. You
see into the house. You see the candles. You watch the people. You can
see what it's like inside. The candles draw you. You get a cold feeling
being outside. Separated. You have an idea that being inside it's
cozier. Warmth. People. Conversation. Everyone using a language.
Then you go inside. It's a shock. It's not like how you expected. You
lose what you had outside. You forget that there even is an outside.
The inside is all you know. You hunt for a way of being with
everyone. A way of finding how to behave . . .*

—Sam Shepard
Shooter, in *Action*

Contents

Selvage Edge

Enterprise, Ohio

Sherwood Anderson Walks Out

"My feet are cold, wet and heavy from long wading in a river.
Now I shall go walk on dry land," I said . . . I went along a spur of
railroad tracks, out of a town and out of that phase of my life.

—A Story Teller's Story

His first day gone, he wanders from the tracks
into a fallow field, its tangled weeds
ripping around his ankles like rotten fabric
and slowing him down. Chilled and winded, he stops
to look things over. Behind him is a city,
its horizon dark as war, and the small factory
he owns and has left mid-letter. To the west a train
huffs its dense progress toward the sunset.
It is the last day of November, 1912.
The glowering sky is broken with yellow light,
the air is sharp and smoke-tinged, and he whispers

to some sparrows, *I am lost.* He laughs
at himself and listens to the laugh fall short.
But there is patience in this countryside,
and when he comes to a makeshift bridge he sits at its edge
and watches the river moving under its clear
new skin of ice. He reaches into his pockets
which are full of field corn and pulls out
a piece of paper, a letter to himself.
Elsinore get to Elsinore, it says.
Keep thinking of that and walk. He folds it, trembling,
his mind a narrow maze, repetitions

of himself trapped like leaves in river ice,
like dreams inside sleep. Beneath them, this dark running.
Not far to the south he sees a modest farmhouse.
Its builder has marked his initials on its roof
with a darker shade of slate. He thinks that roof

is like a poem, an inverted open book,
and that house is the plain, living story.
His heart beats wild wings. He admires this man
living beneath the small roof of his name.
He would like to walk with him in this field,
to put his hand upon the man's shoulder in parting.

He turns toward the northwest, into the wind,
and heads for a little town across the fields.
It's getting late. The land becomes familiar,
jostling his memory. He walks as if unseen
down a dim, cobbled Main Street, and watches
its small parade of lives: a woman clerk
locking up the dime store for the night,
a young man muttering phrases to himself,
a doctor slowly climbing stairs, a teacher
leaving school. They add themselves to him,
In the dark he sees their solitary faces.

His head is full of simple, solid words
as beautiful and neglected as these lives.
They move in a procession and repeat
themselves to him. He sees his life among them.
As he leaves, his mind is piecing a mosaic.
There is only this roof of black midwestern night,
this town beneath it, his forty years, a few
dollars in his pocket, and it is enough.
Something happened, he'll say in a letter, years later.
Anyway I came home and began to write.
I am a man you would not be ashamed to know.

Produce

No mountains or ocean, but we had orchards
in northwestern Ohio, roadside stands
telling what time of summer: strawberries,
corn, apples—and festivals to parade
the crops, a Cherry Queen, a Sauerkraut Dance.
Somebody would block off a street in town,
put up beer tents and a tilt-a-whirl.

Our first jobs were picking berries.
We'd ride out early in the back of a pickup—
kids my age, and migrants, and old men
we called bums in sour flannel shirts
smash-stained with blueberries, blackberries,
raspberries. Every fall we'd see them
stumbling along the tracks, leaving town.

Vacationland, the signs said, from here to Lake Erie.
When relatives drove up we took them to see
The Blue Hole, a fenced-in bottomless pit
of water we paid to toss pennies into—
or Prehistoric Forest, where, issued machine guns,
we rode a toy train among life-sized replicas
of brontosaurus and triceratops.

In winter the beanfield behind our house
would freeze over, and I would skate across it
alone late evenings, sometimes tripping
over stubble frozen above the ice.
In spring the fields turned up arrowheads, bones.
Those slow-plowing glaciers left it clean and flat here,
scraping away or pushing underground what was before them.

Carnies

That's what we went for, Holly and I,
not for the rides or the games we couldn't win.
What were we then, fourteen, fifteen,
wearing cut-offs and our brothers' workshirts.
Holly tossing her hair as we walked down the midway,
her talking big and me saying nothing, a halfstep
behind her. But don't you know how deep summer
crawls inside you in a town like that.
You can't keep still, you need fast
fresh air from another place. And if boys
your own age try showing off for you there,
you nod and shrug but keep glancing away.
You look over at the quick swipes of grease
on the jeans of some muscled roustabout unlocking
the safety bars on the Octopus, you watch
the flutter of his T-shirt, the travel of his eyes.
And when he looks at you you're caught
not knowing what to do, and afraid to smile.
You just move on through that broken-down music.
Holly and I, we took our time getting on
and off those rides, we craved that coolness
just an extra second airborne, scrambling
summer and Main Street and a stranger's level gaze.
And you bet we'd take them home with us,
their soft goddamns that followed us out,
and wouldn't we toss all night with them, too.

Protection

She sees him from the corner
of her right eye, it's his red
damp T-shirt across the street,
the heavy swing of his arms—
that crazy Joe Friend who eats
creamed corn or soup from the can,
signs his name with an *X*, sits
by the tracks counting boxcars.
It's a hazy eight A.M.,
dog day Sunday, and no one
around. He drifts to his left
slow until he's plodding, hands
in pockets, down the center
line of the street, watching her
sideways, his loose walk stumbling
in step to her faster pace
as both of them cut across
the vacant lot. Then he's right
behind, she feels the shadow
of size, and she turns, angry,
shaken, shouts *Leave me alone!*
and he stops, sudden, backsteps
a bit like he'd been shoved by
her voice, or as though her words
were a kind of surprise wall.
And she feels guilty somehow
then, and hurries away. And
he doesn't move until he
forgets. He follows her down
to the highway, she crosses
four fast lanes and he just stands
stopped there again, staring out
like it's water he can't swim.

Assembler

My twentieth summer I got a job in Door Locks
at the Ford plant where my father has worked
for twenty years. Five in the morning
we'd stand tired in the glare and old heat
of the kitchen, my father fiddling with
the radio dial, looking for a clear station.

There weren't any women in my department.
At first the men would ask me to lift
what I couldn't, would speed up the turntable,
juggling the greasy washers and bolts,
winking at each other, grinning at me.
In the break room they would buy me coffee,
study my check to see if I got shorted.
They were glad I was in school and told me
to finish, they said I'd never regret it.
Once I got loaned to Air Conditioners,
worked three days in a special enclosure,
quiet and cool and my hands stayed clean.
Out the window I could see Door Locks,
the men taking salt pills, 110 degrees.

In rest rooms there were women sleeping
on orange vinyl couches, oven timers ticking
next to their heads.

At lunch I'd take the long walk to my father.
I'd see him from a distance, wearing safety glasses
like mine, and earphones, bright slivers of brass
in his hair—him standing alone in strange sulfur light
amidst machines the size of small buildings.
Every twenty minutes he worked a tumbler,
in between he read from his grocery bag of paperbacks.
He would pour us coffee from a hidden pot,
toast sandwiches on a furnace. We sat

on crates, shouting a few things and laughing
over the roar and banging of presses.

Mostly I remember the back-to-back heat waves,
coffee in paper cups that said Safety First,
my father and I hurrying away from the time clocks,
proud of each other. And my last day, moving shy past
their *Good Lucks,* out into 5:00, shading my eyes.

The Reservoir

That summer she pretends to oversleep,
practices looking the other way.
She hadn't planned to come home,
but it was deep habit, no danger,
and maybe some of the endings she needed
might be found, after all, in Enterprise, Ohio.
Mostly she wants a week
that repeats itself, the neutral
color scheme of her bedroom, work
hard enough to make her rest
and deserve it. She is tired
of waking up and waking up.

Days, she works transplanting,
cashiering, at a greenhouse. Evenings,
she shelves books at the library.
The people of Enterprise read mysteries,
westerns, Harlequin romances,
diet books, how-to's, fix-it's.
Sometimes she stands camouflaged
in stifling Number Five House amidst
geraniums, ivies, schefflera, made aware
of her breathing. Sometimes, shelving,
she half-hides in the 800's,
leans against the cool bindings
of Goethe or Plato.

Walking, she passes these signs
all summer—one is painted in red
on a ripped bed sheet and hangs
from an upstairs window:
"You've had it? *You're* the problem!"
And this hand-printed and taped
to someone's front door: "Day Sleeper."
In the Christian bookstore window,

a white-on-black placard: "Does mortality
limit you?"

From the top of the reservoir as she runs
she sees to her right the south edge of town,
then the woods surrounding Raccoon Creek,
the ball diamonds, Fultz's Garage, wheat,
corn, Al's Shop-Rite. And to her left
the blue five-sided water, the dock
they would dive from to break the law,
grim fishing men on the white stones or out
in silver boats. And alongside her, beer cans,
rubbers, torn cardboard, bleached crawdads,
and she runs it again and everyday, for it's only
from this height and pace she can love her town.

I used to follow the train tracks into the country
to be by myself, singing under my breath.
The rails ridged up between the fields
seemed the only elevation, the only road out.
Trains passed through like they were still important
and I'd stand in their wind, reading the flaking names
on old boxcars, Erie Lackawanna, Chessie, Rock Island.
After they passed, the quiet went deeper,
the land lay light green after green, almost seamless.
It wasn't beautiful, exactly, but it was whole,
it was all I knew. As far as I walked
I could turn around and still see the town.

Sometimes she meets high school friends
again. They're always changing
their names. Some have regular
nicknames, like "Moose" or "Mumbles,"
but mostly it works this way: Greg

is called Ernie, Mike is Rick, Gary
becomes Greg. They've done this for years.

That summer even James Dean begins
to look old. She grows impatient
with his fists and stammers. Damp air
loosens the photographs from the walls
and James Dean pointing his finger at her
slips behind the bookcase. Beneath
the nightstand in a loose roll is James Dean
crucified, his arms hooked and limp
over a rifle, his head bowed.

Summer hangs in the trees, in my hair.
I walk slow from the back to the front
of each day and don't recall much,
memory is hard. Time passes this way:
vision jarred to the rise-fall of footsteps,
space taken by words or food in my mouth,
loud people moving in and out of range.
At night the hissing of tires on Maple Street,
long sighs close to my window.
And the far trains, their loose clatter,
their old held-out note—

Some nights she just walks around
inside the house. Above her, her brother
plays his guitar in his bedroom, his bent
blues notes moving over a week's dirty clothes
and pocket change, finding the open windows.

She sways a little in the failing light,
moving in time from window to window.
Watches out at children chasing
and closing their fists over fireflies.

Her mother in passing remarks once
or twice how she should be grateful
she's not married, tied down,
as if that were the subject.
As if they'd been talking.
And she shrugs a nod because it's
a reply. And her mother says Don't
worry, the right boy will come along.

In the dream I'm thinking, You can have
your landslides, *when suddenly
I trip and stumble down
a steep bank tangled with vines thick
as a man's fingers. When I right myself
I'm in a rowboat, on a calm lake misted
dense as fever, all mauve and cool
and blue, Arthurian. I can't see past
the bow or stern. The boat
wants to steer itself, and I let it.*

A letter tells her offhand
he'll be married that August.
In July they meet by accident
and try some talk. She offers
congratulations and catches him
off-guard. He never would have told her.
He doesn't name his fiancée,
just says "she" or "her."
What she notices most is how easily
she lets go of him and ten years—
and also the exclusiveness,
the strange gravity, of his "we,"
how it tops her halting "I's"
the way paper-covers-rock.

Across her street is a small swing park
where she used to play. Even late
at night she hears games, laughter,
coming from behind its trees. Tonight
her brother is singing and playing his guitar
on their porch, sings *The water is wide,*
I cannot get o'er, and neither have I
wings to fly. She leans by the screen door
in the front hall, hums some and stops,
hears how the night holds his song alone.
But from the park comes the working creak
of the merry-go-round, and then she hears
listeners, imagines their faces spinning
silent through the long-winded dark.

She dreams she's back in grade school
taking a test, when her mind goes
blank, and she panics but tells herself
Just concentrate and *Use what you know*
and there'll be an answer, and an A
in the end. But nothing comes, all she hears
is the scratching of pencils,
a roomful of solutions.
She dreams she's sitting on stair steps
with James Dean, but he's her brother,
and is crying, his head on her lap.
She dreams the sky of Enterprise filled
with tornadoes, with colored balloons.
And she wakes everyday between 6:00
and 6:05. She tries, but she has never
been able to oversleep.

The sun is spread thin,
a white glaze of heat.

It makes her tired, walking to work,
and when she reaches the railroad
crossing she just stops,
sits on the tracks. The street is asleep
except for a woman shaking out rugs,
and a thin boy playing. He wears hard
shoes and no socks. This is the street
with the birch tree—a young tree
absolutely straight and balanced,
growing in a sunny sideyard.
Once she sees it she starts walking again.
Everyday she reads its shadow.

In bedroom windows fans buzz
like trapped, silver insects.
Laundry sags from clotheslines.
Familiar faces, day sleepers,
people laid off, lean in alleys
or doorways against brick and rust.
Railroads made this a boom town once.
Most of the tracks are grassed over, the ties
have been sold. They edge driveways and gardens.
This town teaches no one how to leave.
Tonight cars will race
down this street spilling horn blasts,
music, shouts sharp as broken bottles.
The little fans hum in upstairs windows,
outside sprawl climbing roses
bound upright with twine.

It's six A.M., and she's thinking
You've had it? You're the problem!

Just concentrate, use what you know.
And she knows she's been promised
most of her life to one or another
of her secret partners—
Enterprise, leading men, long-range plans
she might never grow to love.
She has distances she wants to try
alone. And still, like anyone,
it's belonging she wants, it's the idea
of *settled* or *permanent address.*
And all she's done has been only so much
rent paid toward that place.

She's outside of Enterprise, running the reservoir,
singing to herself *The water is wide,*
looking past the south and east edges
of town, at the reach of August sky
and black clouds moving quickly
from the west, and she's thinking
Sometimes if I open my eyes very wide
there's this space which is like
room for error. And I see limits,
I see things that can change my mind.
It's what she'll remember most
from this long wedded summer—her orbits
around a five-sided body of water
with usually a storm of some kind in the distance.

Long ago, a teacher had told her
about his genius friend, and how
he'd sit with his thoughts wherever
they came to him, thinking them through,
and how he found him once, drenched,

oblivious, sitting chin-in-hands
on a street corner. And this
was the first ambition she could remember,
to not have sense enough to come in out of the rain.

Used Mysteries

Outings

I remember asking *Why go
for a ride just for a ride? Why walk
through cemeteries reading the stones?*
I was five. We had driven out past their old farm,
then left our cars along the main road—
my aunt, uncle, grandfather, cousins,
my parents. We chewed sassafras roots
my grandfather pulled up and peeled
as we shuffled the hot chalk of the road.
Then we came to two private gardens
of graves, mowed, shaded. Our parents
nodded at some of the names
while we children murmured how pretty
the marble, how long ago the years,
as we edged between where the bodies were buried.

I found my own name and age, a girl
dead in the spring of 1860.
Read her marker aloud in my new-reader voice:
Deborah, 5 years, She hath done what she could.

When I got older I would stay
in the car on our visits to Greenlawn,
where an uncle and cousin had since been taken.
Winter, my sister would sit in my lap.
I remember her asking *Why
do we have to go to this place?*
I said *Because,* our breaths frosting the windows.
And when we drove away she and I drew pictures
on the glass. With gloved fingers
we wrote our autographs and watched
what was passing beyond the spaces
our names had cleared.

Offering

At night in Vinton County a Satanic cult
is sacrificing farmers' calves and lambs.
My grandmother rubs her hands as she speaks of it
in a voice that absently fingers its words
like the tissue her bony hands grip and twist,
the newspaper she smoothes and folds.

My grandfather, hard of hearing, arthritic,
watches a television that doesn't work.
These days he believes raccoons are living
in their house, that they eat right out of his hand.
He grins at us, alert, remote, as she talks,
and points to a dusty plastic fern,
his few words wrestling with silence.

The light of my grandparents' living room
belongs to no hour or season. It is the light
of the parlor—shades drawn, its kept darkness
a preservative, a hush. But as a child, being quiet
is one of the things I am best at, so that adults
might forget I am there and discuss
what I'm not supposed to hear.

On my lap I'm holding the Sunday comics,
a flat blur of simple colors and letters,
and as I feign reading I can see the robed
and hooded figures circling their altar.
I see the lamb, its legs bound, in moonlight
as bright as this room's daylight is dim.

But it's pure television. I can't believe
the Devil is on this farm any more than I
think God resides in our particular church.
What I do understand is the dead live here—
their pictures are everywhere, their pallid breath.

My grandmother rises to cover the bird cage,
reads to herself from the open Bible beside it.

On the end tables are photographs of two sons lost
to war, to accidents. And on the table before me
is the picture I have colored in Sunday school
that morning, and have given to my grandmother.
Blessed are the meek, it says above my black
and blue planet Earth, suspended between God's
white, idle hands, all of it ours to inherit.

Kindergarten Class Picture, 1962

None of us are smiling except for Jeff,
a gap-toothed boy whose sweatshirt shouts GUNSLINGER.
Otherwise, three rows of similar children—
the girls cardiganed and latticed with dark plaid,
the boys thin in the quiet stripes of their shirts—
and Mrs. Hopkins gazes out benignly
from the back row, as slender and unmussed
in her starched housedress as some television mother.

The shortest of us are seated in front of the risers.
We're rigid in wooden chairs, eight pairs of hands
palms-down on knees; we're braced with stillness,
ready for inspection. And no child is more
soldierly than myself, small arms extended
uncomfortably, following instructions to the letter.
I am as strange to me as the twenty other children
I'll never see again after that year—
my stick-straight hair cropped boyish by my mother,
both shins bruised down to anklets. My poker face—
an attentive, absent stare I can't decipher.

If I wanted to guess what happened to these children,
where they were twenty-five years later,
this photograph would provide few clues.
In this picture we are still too much a unit,
facing the moment flashed before us. We're caught—
mean Gary, coy Christine, even Billy,
slow learner, mouth agape—we're mesmerized,
transfixed by that bright, brief light ahead.
It's as pure white as the winter sky behind us,
tall and wide in each bare window,
a nothingness that takes up half the picture.

Children's Story

What I can't tell them is how normal time
sometimes folds just a little in the wind
the way a flag does, changing its picture.
It's like what's happening bends in and out,
but I just keep walking straight. At school once,
the crossing guard held up a Stop bar,
but I slipped under it and stepped out
into the street. The car that was coming
was a police car, and the policeman
stopped, shook his finger at me and frowned,
and everything around me blurred away to each side,
like a chalk drawing on the sidewalk when it rains.
The next day they sent me upstairs to be scolded
by a teacher who was all voice and no words,
no picture. Sounds scraped themselves
inside her throat, sharpening up as they went.
The next time I did it, I stayed home
for three days. I said I was sick
and my mother believed me. I don't mean
to make all these mistakes, it's just
I have other eyes looking someplace else.

Next-Door Neighbors

Grant Street was one long Sunday afternoon
in February or March, a few yards of brown grass
thinning and matted, or rubbed away hard.
Our house stayed dark with my mother's pleurisy,
and it made me angry, the way she kept trying
to raise herself up to clean rooms or fix supper.
Then she'd lie down again on the couch, covering
herself tight with two blankets, chilling.
It was Sunday afternoon, foggy, and my father
was playing his Hank Williams record.
He's dozing at the end of the couch, his hand
on my mother's feet, and I go outside to sit
on the porch. Mr. Carter from across the street
pulls up grinning on his Harley and asks me
if I want to take a ride, and I do, but I don't
like his eyes, and besides, I'm not allowed to,
and shake my head no. I'm ten or eleven
with a younger brother and sister somewhere,
but my seeing is short-ranged and telescoped—
cardboard taped to the Carters' front window,
the busted taillight on our old white Comet,
yesterday's *Register*, "The World at Your Doorstep."

Mrs. Carter appears in the broken-paned window,
another black eye, and pulls down the blind.
My mother had called Mrs. Carter to ask if
she'd come over and blow cigarette smoke into her earache,
she had read somewhere that it helped.
But Mrs. Carter said sorry, she couldn't leave the house.
I'd yelled at my mother then why didn't she go
to a doctor, I slammed the door and was sorry.
Now I'm sitting on the step, biting the polish
off my nails. I don't like my coat, it's reversible
and has imitation fur. The snow edging the empty street
looks like coal. Next year Mr. Carter will go

to the electric chair for killing an old man
and his wife and hiding their pieces in his car trunk.
One night I'll forget to kiss my father goodnight
before he drives off to the factory with just one
taillight working, and I'll worry to sleep seeing that,
certain he'll die. I pray for goodness
and mercy every night, I want too many things.

Twelfth Thanksgiving

The plain, stiffening dark of late November,
a country day, dulled cold and gray as pewter,
and dinner delayed, my father working late.
I stepped outside at dusk, its rustled chill
parting my hair, my open coat, and walked
beyond the garden's idle wreckage, the grass
tough and pale beneath my loose-laced boots.
And far into the fields I turned around
to face our house, the steamed yellow windows
of the kitchen where my mother's shadow moved
about the table, and saw my father pull up—
the gentle incline of his silhouette
walking toward the side door, disappearing
into the house. And there was absolutely
nothing that I needed on this earth
that I did not have. My bare hand reached to touch
the milkweed tall beside me, not to disturb
or scatter, just connecting, holding on.

Getting Religion

1.

Back then I prayed nights
out of the same superstition
that kept me from using
the coffee table Bible
as a coaster. Made me sleep

with hands hidden because I read
in some waiting-room book of *Bible Stories
for Children* about a sick boy
who propped his hand up one night
as a sign he was ready, and later Jesus,
making his hospital rounds,
saw him and took him up on it.

I went to church every Sunday.
There was a boy there I liked—
an elder's son, a neglected
practical joker who slipped
his hand over mine during prayers.
But sometimes it was Jesus

I was looking for, exploring
the closed stairway and back rooms
of our House of God.
And where I felt his presence most
and liked him best was down

in the basement's back hallway,
past the kitchen where my mother
and I measured out communion wafers,
past the Sunday School rooms
and the cracked varnish of *Christ
on the Road to Emmaus,*

where that boy and I practiced
kissing after choir. It was dark
and drafty, the smooth brick walls
were cold, and all those old wooden doors
would rattle soft in their frames,
restless Jesus wandering the halls again.

2.

A few of us stood scattered in the pews to sing
early on summer Sundays, before church,
in the first light strained milky olive and brown
through a triptych of somber stained glass.
I was the only one there under fifty,
and I was thirteen, skeptical but trusting,
God's repentant orphan and contralto.
I was there for the low pleasant drone
of redemption, the slow scoops of old voices
through seven or eight verses, their words worn
into the music like footsteps into marble stairs.
Some of the others didn't even use hymnals,
but sang in rote praise all the way to Amen,
blind persons on the arm of someone leading them home.
There was no plan, no leader, whoever
wanted to said *198* or *316,* and we sang
Blest be the tie that binds, we sang,
beneath the heavenly descant of silence,
Have thine own way Lord, have thine own way.

3.

What I knew about my father was he worked—
a graduate, he'd laugh, of the school
of hard knocks. I couldn't imagine him at church
or praying, like Mr. Miller or Mr. Brown,
eyes closed, hands folded idle in his lap.
Though once he decided to go to adult Sunday school,
and went regularly for a couple of months.
Most of the class, I knew, were middle-aged
women who organized bazaars, spaghetti or
pancake suppers; and hatted old ladies
whose lipstick colored in and outside of the lines,
and whose voices likewise trailed a second behind
everyone else in unison prayers.

Our own class was spent in memorization
and reading Bible comics. What did my dad do,
I worried, maybe he'd never gone to church before.
But those women and their quiet, suited husbands
would surprise me with their hugs after sermons
or in the choir room, exclaiming what a delight
my father was, what wonderful stories he told,
what jokes. Then for months they'd be asking me
to tell him to come back, the Sunday school needed him.
I didn't doubt that, and I'd stand there, nodding,
picturing him at home on his only morning off,
working in our garden, or dozing by the TV,
hand keeping his place in another used mystery.

Background, 1969

After our early move two hundred miles north
of the Ohio River there were weekend trips
to what my parents called Down Home.
Sunday night meant the long drive back,
hours of talk, fast food, and radio—
country stations I found as embarrassing
as the front yards full of rust-gutted cars
in the hillbilly hollows we had left behind,
but rock from Detroit as we got further north.
I sang those songs with an edgy reverence,
anthems of an exclusive club I joined underage,
but as far from my life as *Easy Rider*.
Being the oldest guaranteed me a window,
and I watched that worn landscape repeating itself
as plaintive and predictable as any steel guitar,
as much my soundtrack, my relative, as any.
Eventually we just passed those miles
in cramped, uneven sleep, holding
to the hum of tires and front-seat murmurs.
Woke confused at gas stations or stoplights,
though a glance told us how much farther.

Once, in the wide flat black of October,
when only my father and I were awake,
a few seconds separated us from being
slammed broadside by a car that came flying
dark and low out of nowhere, and skimmed
swift and streamlined as chance itself
through the unlit intersection just ahead.
My father, a calm man, barely blinked
and kept driving. My sisters' small
faces were untroubled in their sleep.
I settled back, shaken, but I didn't
say anything, and already I had begun
to doubt what I had seen. My reflection

looked back at me, mine and not mine,
in the dark window of our sleep-hushed car,
moonlit Ohio running behind
my ghosted face in the glass, as I leaned
my own black flight of dreams against it.
Against the rushing reversible order
of cornfields and Main Streets, against the whole
landlocked silent movie of the Midwest.

In Transit

What Is Called For

I walk in old shoes through the melting snow.
My shoes and socks are soaked. The sun is shining,
a white March glint, a squinting eye.
I too am always squinting when I walk.
The streets are steep here. I enjoy their steepness,
the visible, short-term task they represent.
They lead me to the main street, which is wider
and grander than seems necessary. Ionic columns
stand isolated, bare, supporting nothing.
Walking around, one senses absences,
as if most of the people who normally reside here
are missing, have been called away.
All the stores are open, their windows filled
with faded items—books, bolts of fabric,
small signs washed white by the sun's long stare.
Mannequins face the street in poses of welcome
or indifference, but the parking spaces
stay empty—their meters waiting, straight as sentries,
to count down an hour. The local papers change
or stay the same. I stop, bend, try to read them
in their vending machines, read the windowed
stories and headlines and cannot understand
the references or why they are important.
Where do the stories happen in this vacant place?
I repeat the city's name to myself,
its syllables a whisper blown behind me.
Am I more north or less north than the place
where I was last? How long shall I stay here,
how long have I stayed? A month? A year?
Will it be over soon, is it nearly over?
And what about what's next—what waits for me—
should I be planning yet, or anxious about it,
or calm, or stolid? What is, in fact, called for?
The reader might recognize these questions—
they are tall, well-dressed, polite, insistent.

These questions quickly fill the tiny room
in which I am staying, so I excuse myself
to go for a walk. I walk up and down the steep streets
of a city that seems foreign to me, and empty.
The shops are open, but I do not enter anywhere,
I just keep walking, focusing my concentration
on crossing streets where no cars are coming,
walking when the light tells me to Walk.
I think about my feet being cold and wet,
or the sun melting the black debris of snow.

Money

The young woman in the yellow coat
comes into the laundromat to get warm
and to get change for the damp dollar
she's saved. Most Sunday mornings,
when she and I are here like clockwork,
she only pretends to spend, standing
in front of the detergent vending machine,
raising her quarter to the coin slot
and then jerking it away, stepping back
and then up again, lifting her money,
repeating it all with minced
nervous steps, as if someone put a coin
in her to do just that, as if time
draws a sudden line she can't live past.

But this morning, whether by accident
or intent, the change falls through,
and she clasps her toy box of All
to her breast and leaves. When she opens
the door all the hand-lettered signs,
which are posted above washers and say NO DYING!
flap up and wave. I watch her split shoes
do their tiptoed two-step,
forward, reverse, idling, across
the iced street to the corner grocery,
where she waits by the Closed sign,
huddling in place. I see her there

each morning when I'm walking
to work. Usually she'll have a dollar
folded sharp in her hand, trying
in her skittish way to jimmy the lock,
or she'll be pressing the bill

against the door like a pass
and peering inside. *Mean woman,*
her breath fogs the glass, her teeth chatter,
you mean woman open the door please.

Tour of Duty

In his dream he tells himself *Mouths to feed,*
though the gun he shoulders is an infantry rifle,
a souvenir of his father's from World War II.
And when he steps outside he finds himself

in Sweden again, hitching a ride,
his mouth full of aliases, false life stories.
He dreams he's looking for work.
He joins a carnival as a ride operator

and stays until the looping screams drive him
into a small arcade. He feeds quarters
to a glass-caged chicken who dances
while pecking at an electrified piano.
Then he remembers what he had set out to do,

remembers his wife and children.
The children are hers. They tug at his arm.
His wife—he can't tell if it's the first one
or the second—is slamming cupboard doors in the kitchen.
She says there are mouths to feed, and he shouts

You know I would kill for them!—And he would,
he wants to. He grabs the gun and goes back
into the woods, shoots down something small,
and guts and skins it while the children watch.
Her boy says *Now his head doesn't make any noises.*

Walking Below Zero You Tell Yourself

I am just another breath here.

This arctic night's mirages want
to take you home now,
take you in. For a moment

the razored wind becomes a roof
or cave, then it crashes down.
For a moment the wind is a siren,
a lying lullaby that would keep you
rocked in its barren insides.

It's true what they say,
that after so long
in this weather you just want to sleep.
The mind lets go of its moorings,
one by one, and begins to lose you.
It says, *The snow is safe and warm,*
says, *This is a good place to stop.*

But you grip your short life
like a towrope, you move
in the direction of your own voice.
You think, to keep alive. You walk
in as straight a line as you can.

Somewhere you remember a dance
from before you were born,
remember it the way your body remembers
the child you haven't conceived yet—
Your parents circling
through the bright rush of some folk dance—

But then the light of that goes out.
You think, *It is almost too cold for light.*

Between blasts are the feverish scatterings
of stars, the fixed dark windows of houses.

At the edge of town the wind dies.
The stillness here is before everything.
You want to go on, into the trees.

A Little Blessing

A little blessing might have deflected it.

—Arthur Miller

I was with the other women in the changing-room
after our concert. This was ten years ago.
We were taking off identical black dresses
when one of the women let out a soft, sharp cry
when she saw me, how I looked undressed.
Your little body, she said, almost a whimper.
And I pretended not to hear, but that stranger's sound
broke a private mirror, it broke a spell.
I have pictures of me then, all sparrow bones,
my hair a dead ash-blonde. I think I wanted
to just kite through that time, my skin as thin
as an airmail envelope, the translucent blueness
of my pure soul showing through. I think
that was what I wanted. I don't remember.

I still resist the dulling ballast of food,
but I take it in. I obey the random call
of hunger, that spoiled child, that bad parent.
I can't imagine how it was before.
At least now I can bear to have a body,
a home for this irrevocable confusion.
What I like about my life is one room contains it.
It's spare and clean. I understand this room,
but the world outside has always been beyond me.
I don't know how it works, what holds it up.

And I don't know how the people move about,
combining and separating like complex traffic.
And marriages—how easily they fall
in and out of them, those busy houses,
thresholds being crossed like finish lines.

And then the children being born and needing,
their long cries falling into languages.

In the morning I watch children go to school.
Parents' cars drive up and drive away—
each child alone, and then alone with others,
shuffling in their mismatched caps and layers
toward the door. I smile at them,
I walk right through them,
and they don't see me. Sometimes I want
to hold one in my arms, sing one to sleep.
I'd be so good, so careful. But that feeling
is as nameless as my hunger, and goes away.
I'm thirty. I need a word to keep me here.
My watch, at its last notch, turns on my wrist,
the hour ticking up against my pulse.

Sentiment

This is not about me.
This is about someone else,
from some other winter. A boy
I knew once. He was poor then,
living on the outskirts of town,
and the blowing snow would sift under
the warped sashes in his bedroom,
so that when he woke there
would be snowflakes dusted light
as dreams, light as his dead
mother's kisses, on his hair,
on his thin blue wool blanket,
his shirt. He told me this
was true and I believed him.

I just wanted to give him
what he didn't have. What I
didn't have. I wanted to press
his cold lips with the small
exact promise of my kiss,
saying *I will never
leave you.* But that wasn't
what he wanted, not then.
And yet, years later, adrift,
he still sifts into my dreams,
a chill and coarse light,
and he lies down beside me,
too tired to explain, and I warm
him until he can sleep.

New Flower Rules

On Water Street, the humming of pink neon,
the false fronts of shops forever changing names.
She likes the sleek *noir* gleam of the cruising cars,
the backlit group of boys across the street,
their laughter shifting, defining them in the twilight.
August, the air clad with something tarnished.

She turns left, heads back into the sullen town,
the damp dime store perfume of flower beds,
the skeletal light of television in rooms
where a child rocks back and forth counting to ten,
or a couple's shouts fall from an open window
over the soulless stares of toys left out in yards.

A dirt road leads up to the cemetery.
The entrance has a sign, *New Flower Rules,*
warning when a clean sweep will be made
of all grave decorations. The moon is full
and low, a dusky orange. She likes the soft give
of cinder, and the names' fleet *Quebecois:*

Thibodeau, LeClair. And *Anne and Marie Dulac,*
"Mother and Daughter, Faithful to the End"—
two tablets merging halfway down, their years
effaced. She bends to pull some Queen Anne's lace
from their grave. Sits awhile in that moonlit spot
above the risen light of public places.

Then downhill to the bridge, its rough, wide arc
of granite warm beneath her hand. The river
is dazed and slow, leaf-dusted, black.
She leans over, looks down at no reflection,
lets go the weed and watches its sluggish progress.
Clean sweep, she says, *clean sweep,* and likes the sound.

Self-Defense

Charles Starkweather, 1958

1. Lincoln, Nebraska

I had a few plans.
They come to me when I was still driving
the garbage truck. I'd write them down
on paper I folded into airplanes,
then I'd fly them into the landfill.

Caril and me, later, we'd write
notes on scrap paper of all
what we'd done and toss them
out the car window.

Carrying dirt from one place
to another enough times
will drive a man crazy,
my daddy always said.

It was like my brain got lost
in my head. I couldn't stop
to think about little
or big, things was going
on fast. The ones I killed
already murdered me, murdered
me slow some and I was kinder
to them, killed them in a hurry.

2. In Prison They Give Him a Dictionary and a Bible

Mrs mott tolded us then the first day
of school to tell are hobbys My turn
i begin to speak, my voice was smearing
faint and cracked, the kids they bursted
in to laughter, i flinch, startle, flaccid
lacking in firmness, then was completely
flabbergast as my words became flat as
i started to speak again i sadden
they had no regard for my feelings

And i left, sat on a little chair
inside the playhouse, sat staring
out the window, glaring antagonists,
pinioned thus, strained toward kids in the room,
and it seemed i could see my heart
before my eyes turning dark
black with hate of rages
stripped from this life leaving
only naked being-hate

3. He Confesses Seven Times

Sometimes Death would come to me
like a long train whistle,
or a shape at my window, half-human,
half-bear. Once he come to me
with a coffin and we sailed in it,
down a river of fire that was cold.

He tries to hug me in my cold again now
but i took holt of both his arms, i shove

him good   My head then smote and my teeth
chattered violence and my hands
cold as Death and my body burning
And i slept then finely after a week
of not sleeping   i slept and there was
dream after busy dream of these
i remember nothing and am glad

Things was just waiting
for me to get to them, that's all.
Sometimes my brain feels close
to explode, they set me spinning
with all their do-good captivities
and hurry-up voices, they make me feel
like I'm nothing but a bunch
of talking shadows, staggered tied
loose together not matched, not moving
together at the same time, not fitting.

Maybe there were some good
people here but they weren't
good for me. It might
have been different but it wasn't.
I'm what wasn't, I guess.

And caught here i am just to discard
now that i am confessed nearly broke
and are dogged, all of them tugging
Earthbound my soul

And maybe the next world is more
like the one I wanted, always
I wished I could just go hunting
in forests again away where

they can't bother me at last
and live with the animals
and trees in the majesties
of our Lord Jesus Christ.

4. Badlands

So it would make me happy
if everbody will just go on
like anything didnt happen
but im not real sorry
for what i did cause for the first
time me and Caril had more
fun she help me a lot
But if she comes back dont
hate her she had not much
to do with the Killings   Look
all we wanted to do is
get out of town

I used to walk by the restaurant
of the Cornhusker Hotel and look
in at those fine people and
think there it is, the world
I hate. And that's how I feel about
these writers, reporters, telling me wrong
in the magazines and newspapers,
they've got my words all fixed
and turned. I'm the only man
who can tell my story, who is
the story about anyhow? Maybe
I'll burn my words so they can't
touch them, maybe I'll lock the pages

in a case and somebody can bury it
and I'll just spend the rest
of my time here not talking, just
looking out my window at what's
out there and stops.

Good Friday

To attempt to speak of what has been would
be impossible. Abyss has no Biographer—

—Emily Dickinson

Each morning I raise the shade
of this upstairs window. Today, the last snow,
the last comment of a closed-mouthed winter.
It falls down fine and straight as rain
on the freezing mud and sloped roofs of the town,
on the thinning gray glass of a nearby river
and the ice fishermen's doorless shanties
pushed back now along the shore, all glazed
and vacant stares, abandoned. They're huddled
but separate, like a crowd of men hoping for work.

Last night, I couldn't escape my dream.
A young boy, about eight or nine years old,
was gunned down during a church service.
Everyone witnessed it—the minister, congregation—
and the police appeared instantly to arrest
the murderer. Then everyone left,
except me, and the dead boy, and someone else—
a peripheral presence, a white glimpse of light
going out. Then suddenly the child leapt up
alive. And I picked up the revolver from the floor
and fired it. He fell just as he was reaching
the door. My clouded mind raced
with how to cover it up—I wiped the prints off
the gun, threw it down. I looked at my hands
in disbelief, and, trembling, dutiful,
sat down to await retribution. I thought
I could say what they always say: *something*
just snapped at that casual resurrection.
That it broke a single dry twig of reason,
the way he undid death, shrugging it off

as if it were a thick blanket in summer.
But after my shot he just lay there,
finished. The silence had an awful
forgetfulness, and I knew no one

was coming back for either of us, ever.
My conscious self began to scramble
for the nearest exit, and I woke in terror
several times, but couldn't shake off the dream—
each time I fell asleep I fell back
into the church. I'd still be sitting
where I had left myself—but the church
had grown into a cathedral around me,
all stone walls and one high stained-glass window,
and the pews had vanished, the altar was gone.
I sat down on a small block of stone
beside the child in our vast mausoleum.

This morning the dream still goes on
in real time. I can feel its chill passing
like a draft I can't locate, rattling doors
I don't usually open. I remember

a home where I was kept for a while.
This was years ago, when I still tried to belong.
I was looking after their baby,
and, nervous, I dropped him
just as the mother came in, and her gasp
hit me like the flat of her hand. She lifted him
and ran out the back door, she stood rocking him
on the frozen slope of their yard,
raising him into the shock of the wind.
I waited on the stoop, thinking *Breathe,*
breathe, the March gusts making sharp turns

on the air, knocking the wind back into all of us,
hard. I watched the weathered clothespins gripped
like wooden acrobats to the trembling line.
Then the mother's skirts billowed and the baby's
red scream rose like the wind turned inside out.
I sank down with my thin prayer still clutched
tight between my two irresponsible hands.

I remember no breast.
I remember my mother
had pale, straight eyelashes,
gray eyes that looked away.

All I have is my story, a simple construction—
a little house you see repeating itself
with variations, street after street.
I've tried to keep my life quiet, spare—
a contained existence, like that of a woman
who is born and dies in her father's house.

But I lived in a blur of foster homes
full of people needing to tell me their secrets,
as if, since I would never talk, I must always
be listening. And I would try to listen—
until my head would be so full of voices
I'd pray, like some crazed telepath, for silence.
I'd pray for rescue, strength, ordinary things.
And would imagine my voiceless nightly petitions
traversing space for years like starlight
until, faint, belated, they would finally fall,
confused with the prayers of others, into
the infinite ear of God.

In the dream, when the boy jumped up, he laughed—
some bright, brief melody lighter than air,
like an invisible colored balloon let go.
It rose through the empty chamber of the dream,
bumped against its granite ceiling.

I have an old photograph somewhere—
me in a secondhand Easter dress,
a gray garden of tulips printed on its skirt.
And I'm wearing a white hat, its thin elastic band
tight beneath my chin, and there's a bow
on the back of it which blows around my face.
One hand clutches the dress—the other, blurred,
brushes away the bow as I squint
in the stark eclipse-light of Good Friday.
I have a memory from the day of that snapshot,
of me running, frightened, slashing noon's
thick veil of stillness with a pinwheel.
I remember the toy's whipped, muted jingle
as the dark wind picked up and it started to rain.

I have wanted to believe in a personal savior.
I've had the idea of heaven inside me
as a place where you didn't have to wait anymore,
a place without inside or outside.

I knew a woman who was especially nice
to any thirtyish man with long brown hair and a beard
just in case he was Jesus come back as promised.
If I was Jesus I would stay where I was,
peripheral and quiet, at a safe distance,
framed within some high stained-glass window.
Sending down his blanket forgiveness
like this snow, covering our rusting wrongs for a while.

In the dream I touched the boy's blond hair,
I bent over him and held his hand. His body was whole,
unharmed, silent. Silent and bloodless as the dream.
I whispered *my fault,* and the words echoed oracular,
then collapsed and widened into nothing.

I'd like us to be lifted, healed, our breaths
given up in a word more perfect than *yes.*
I know some faiths are born
of waiting, of some ragged hope
that's like journeying for days without sleep.
Your nerves stretch slow to a bright
brittle wire, a tightrope your mind walks
until the sheer need for rest becomes
belief, and you let yourself fall.

Maybe God does lift your transparent soul
from the dull rented room of your body,
lifts you erased like the clear plastic page
from a child's slate. Maybe he does
wash you purer than snow, your past
and identity rinsed away with your sins,
then he joins that distillation of you
with all the other anonymous spirits—
And you become the face of the waters he moves on,
you become his very word.

The snow is rain now, I hear it. Spring.
The river's ice will break apart, clouds will loosen
with light. Soon people's voices will come out
of their houses, their tossed conversations
like empty swings tangling in the wind.

From here those fishermen's shanties look
like a child's forgotten alphabet blocks.

One of them is bright blue on one side
and patched with a piece of printed cardboard,
a large black letter *A*. I see myself walk
from this room to the river, each of my small breaths
lost in the air, snow into an ocean.
I go into the windowless box of this pure
open vowel and sit down on a crate.
I wait there, on the frozen face of the river,
while inside me, back in the dream, the walls
of the cathedral grow wider, damp and cold.
They round themselves into a cave, and at its mouth
is silence, a stone I can't roll away.

Possible Endings

1. Swan

Three days after my death in a plane crash
I return to my hometown.
I wander the empty city streets
until nightfall, trying to remember
which train I should take.
At a crossing a strange noise
makes me turn around. A wounded swan,
a knife plunged into its breast,
thin tracings of blood on its white feathers.
It moves toward me, a beseeching look
in its black eyes, and I understand
it wants me to pull out the knife.
I kneel down and take hold—it's odd
how the creature's eyes lock onto mine,
trusting, like a child's—I pull,
and the weapon isn't a knife, after all,
but a tool of some sort,
with a wide, round blade.

I lift the swan and carry it home
to my parents' house. Inside, the gravity
is wrong, is too much, and I lie down,
telling my parents I'm tired,
that I've come home to rest. My mother
makes a bed for the swan in a box.
That's what she tells me as her hands
smooth my blankets, but I hear their
hovering voices later, murmuring
about the dead bird I'd carried home.
I fall asleep and when I open my eyes
I'm lying on an airport runway.
It's night, snow is falling,
thick white flakes. I'm wondering

how much longer I'll have to go on
remembering. My body feels unbearably heavy
with memory. There is a field
in the distance I would like to reach,
but it's far and I tell myself
this red runway light beside me
will do just as well. I close my eyes,
the snow covering me like down.

2. Transport

In death we look like ourselves unharmed
We're wearing our usual clothes
We can see one another but are invisible to the living

A group of us have gathered at a city bus station
A mother and her baby, several students, some older people

We're invisible but we still take up space
We're waiting for a bus with enough empty seats
It's understood we want to travel together

As time passes there's a sense of decay about us
Our clothes get dirtier, tattered, as if they've aged decades
Our faces become sallow, their dark circles deepen
Our lips drained of color, hair thinning, falling
We still carry the other world with us
Out of habit or reluctance we pretend we're still alive
Say we're tired or hungry, missing the needs of the body
The mother tries to nurse the baby but he refuses
He's the most horrifying of us, he has so little to remember

We give up on buses and walk to the airport
It's a small place, mostly commuter planes
We walk as a group across the tarmac to the terminal
Listening to the announcements of arrivals and departures

Somehow the woman at the ticket counter can see us
Are *all* of you dead? she inquires, impressed
We're smiling
There's a great deal of camaraderie among us
Yes, we're nonpersons, says one, grinning and nodding
We have ceased to be, another laughs, raising his eyebrows
We've been *Thanatopsissed,* a third adds, inspired
Prompting a general round of laughter and applause
Even the airline representative joins in

3. Pearls

The end begins with unmarked airships
gliding, silent and impossibly low—
stretched long and black as limousines
above the power lines and trees.
We all come out of our houses to gaze
at the sky in wordless wonder.
We're innocent this way a few minutes.
Then I notice opalescent hailstones
lying like pearls in the grass.

This is the peaceful part, the bodies
just folding earthward in gentle collapse.
Slowly, like undermined buildings.
But plenty of us survive the fallout
to realize the planes have landed
and unloaded soldiers. Some of them
wear gas masks, and others have faces

disfigured into gas masks—leathery,
snouted, speaking some hybrid
and mutated language we all understand.

They have come to individually
finish us with guns—not explosions,
just one person killing one person,
everywhere. A bullet enters above my right eye,
but I'm still lucid, not even shaken.
Are you suffering? the soldier asks,
raising his gun, but I wipe my eye
and with polite and frightened dignity ask
if I may have five minutes more. So he looks away,
lets me wander into the scattershot
silencing of this anonymous town.

It occurs to me then I should choose a place
to die, someplace where I could be alone.
I pass through several deserted rooms
and each of them looks like mine.
In one I find a silver pistol. It feels
cold and good in my hand.
But suddenly it seems ridiculous,
planning where or how I leave my body.
It's out of my hands, I say to myself.
In the end I want to be with everyone.
I put the pistol down and walk
back outside, into the yellow-gray light.

When the bullet hits me from behind
I feel it travel from the base of the cranium

and lodge in the center of my skull.
The pain is gone faster than thought
and I feel my spirit passing from me
like a warm and distant stream of words.
I'm surprised to see the next world open,
an empty and widening transom of light,
and I think, as my self begins to splinter,
that even my enemy, being human,
will want to know that it's there.
So I reach to speak, but my last words
are not my idea: *Father into thy hands.*

Selvage Edge

Stone Soup

*This is the kind of light
that makes you hungry
for structure.*

—Rickie Lee Jones

There's a sleep you pull on like a jacket
that's too thin and small, and the night
invites itself deep into your bones.
In the first breaths of that waking the forgotten
you dream over and over lies cold
and intimate beside you, and you try
so hard to recognize it, it disappears.

It's easier, you tell yourself, to do without.
Easier to keep your ownings contained in one room,
your thoughts no wider than a week
at the outside. Inside, all you need to know
beats in its rib cage or curls upstairs into sleep,
and you travel light; moving, you keep
to the selvage edge of your life.

A man like this might hitch the interstates
like a folk hero, changing his name and story
in each town he jumps into, moving
to the next meal, next odd job, next bed.
A woman like this might move
from rented room to rented room, a quiet boarder,
her few boxes of bare keepsakes
the fixed and shifting natural elements
of her life. And if this man and woman

met each other bent toward the same light
they might discover they share
a language, and in speaking it open the mouth
of something they'll have to feed for years.

This is an old story, and people will pay
to hear about it, always. It has to do
with the storage of the heart, the hunger
we're willing to risk on the outside
chance of getting home.

False Starts

for J., 1954–1975

1. Some Dreams Explain

We're swimming in the quarry
at night, a current works around us.
You step from the water dry. I stand
in the shallows, chilling, watching
you walk away in full moonlight.

We're under gnarled trees, raking leaves
into small piles. The damp, smoky air
that surrounded our argument now clings
to our silences, holds them in place.
I'm wishing warmer coats for us both.

Your mother carries a lamp
through the house, leading me upstairs
to a bedroom. The children asleep
on the bed are you and I, curled toward
each other like hands cupping a prayer.

Last night you approached,
holding a tiny golden pear in your palm.
This was the culprit, you laughed,
shaking your head. *They knocked this out
of my mouth and I came back to life!*

I dreamed a card game.
This is how you play: Put the cards
in your mouth. On each card is a word.
Now take them out, one by one,
place them faceup in order.
Sometimes they make sense.

2. Fall

We get separated in a carnival maze
of mirrors, and what I think is you
is glass, a carousel of your image.
One of you takes a step toward me,
then freezes, fluttering, jammed between frames,
cropped at a hard angle and blurred.

It's your voice that wakes me and holds me still—
your vague and restless blame that hangs
in the air, as if you just left the room.
September returns you, the month you swore
you'd finally leave town for good.
Started your truck, kept the garage door down.

I've dreamed this wild horse before,
I've ridden him. But tonight I see him
flying through fire, and I scream out,
I cry when he lands mottled with burns
and blinded, part of both his forelegs missing.
I put my arms around his raw neck,
not sure if he can even feel or hear me,
and whisper *Everything's going to be all right.*
He stands still as I gently attach
wooden legs, which turn into flesh and bone.

3. Shadow Box

This is almost all I have to say here.

A boy once gave me his jacket
to mend. I made neat, tiny stitches,
I slept holding it close. Sometimes
he'd slip my arms inside it.
Its sleeves fell past my hands.
He would squeeze my hand for good-bye, then leave
me notes in a wild, jagged script.

The night he died I dreamed him reaching
to break off a piece of the sky.
It was brittle as ribbon candy or ice
and melted in my hand. He called
as he drove away, *Don't stop writing me.*

In a wooden cigar box I keep his notes,
some torn tickets, a playing card, motel
matches, a threaded button. *Souvenir,*
he'd say, closing my fingers over it.

Some things you just can't save.
I thought if I dealt with enough details
I'd find the sense that linked them,
complete our sentences. But remembering
only makes more loose ends. I empty
the cigar box and rearrange its contents
as if they might spell some new word.

Composition

*Sometimes for me composition has to do with a certain brightness
or a certain coming to restness . . .*

—Diane Arbus

His story is all place names
out of sequence. Poles, equators,
a litany of flight. In her mind
his past becomes a single city,
far-flung architectures superimposed.

This is what she hears, too,
in his music—in its smash,
its calculated warring.
And in its silence, the sound
of a hand that's raised to strike.

Her words weave. Unweave.
They do not travel.
Behind her halting voice he sees
a narrow stretch of road, a view for miles.
The outlines of a house, one window lit.

When she was a child she used to dream
her body rising to the ceiling
of her bedroom. She could look down
and watch herself asleep below
as if she were her own guardian angel.

As a boy he tossed his head
from side to side to fall asleep—
a wordless, lulling *no,*
a metronome beating time
against disturbance.

When he does this now she watches,
still, beside him, until he calms
and his arms close around her.
The music at rest in the small bones
of his hands sings her toward sleep.
She breathes the wakeful
cadence of all she withholds
into his dreams.
Between them, the sustaining
dissonance of trust.

In the Dream She Doesn't Tell Him

In the dream she doesn't tell him, another snowfall
has begun, and she, lover of cold
and clouds, walks into it, heart-sunk, finally

weary of this winter that will not end.
In the next blink she stands at his apartment.
A note addressed to her is pinned to the door.
Inside it says only *You are loved.*

She opens the door but no one is there.
The apartment is white, bare, trapezoidal,
no curtains, nothing on the walls. Outside
are tall buildings, all new, all vacant.
He walks in behind her then, and suddenly

his ex-wife appears before her.
The two women discover they look just alike.
They face each other and laugh politely.
The small room resonates with the man's unspoken
You are loved, but the woman no longer

believes it's for her. She moves to the door,
eyes down, embarrassed, saying *Thank you,
Good-bye,* knowing when she leaves
the ex-wife, too, will disappear with her

into the thin, exhausted snow of the city,
into the unnamed streets of the city—
will disappear with her. Where no one lives.

House-Sitting

Each day was the unlocking and locking
of doors, the letting in or out
of a cat's fluid shadow, the sorting
of mail addressed to someone else.
Early, I'd walk down to the beach, then back,
to weed the garden, shove a rusty push mower
over patches of scorched, stubborn grass.
And each night hundreds of starlings would roost
in the ornamental trees behind the house,
their concert a cold, shredded breeze.
The cat left their eyeless carcasses
by the shrubs, and in the morning I'd try to sweep
black feathers from the side porch and steps,
but they'd just lift and settle. In the house

the cycles of watering and dusting, the stares
of framed faces becoming familiar.
The thick mirrors caught and startled me—
my face made strange by strange surroundings,
its shadows slowly forgetting the shapes
that had cast them. And one day *his* face
gone from mine, after years—just vanished,
as simply as if I had breathed his name
on the glass. I watched my eyes,
black feathers lifting, settling—*Good-bye,*
good-bye. It was easy. And why not
this address now, why not inhabit this?
Chill salt air blew in through the windows,
healing me beyond recognition.

Two Last Poems for L.

1. Memory

What I remember is his knocking
on my door unexpectedly, early dark
and winter gusts following him in,
his smile pulled tight from the cold.

I see that over and over again.
Him stamping the last bit of snow
from his boots, his clear blue eyes
fixing on mine, *Sorry. Sorry.*

Then the stiff language, the new lie
of his numb hands. Eyes asking
the question they would leave behind.
The shaken exhale of my name.

2. Dream

I was washing his corpse. His skin
looked translucent, his body just as
I remember it. Same misshapen nail
on his index finger, same depression
near the breastbone from childhood polio.
I bathed him slowly, my face a calm mask,
the stopped currents of his strength
trembling through me like light.
How it warmed me to trace his lines again!—
my body shocked awake with love, longing.
I pressed my head against the silent hollow of his chest,
my fingers closed over his closed hand.

Forgiveness

Where you are the temperature plummets
at night, and you sleep in the open
and just gravity holds you. The dry riverbeds
are both penance and reward. I know you've walked
miles now, and you've scattered the last of me

into the pines and box canyons and dust,
into whatever the wind carries and loses,
into a country whose language I don't speak.
So the thoughts you send me now become gestures,
hands pocketed and unpocketed before you move on,

and in my dreams you take on a terrible solidity.
You wear the guilt-laced anger I've seen men mask—
like an old lover of mine who whispered through his embrace,
Omit me from what you have written. You I omit
the way an artist draws with an eraser,

absence taking tangible shape from the darkness.
Whether each of us has exiled within ourselves a memory
we can trust to find its way, or one crippled with lies,
we're learning that the fugitive past can cover
its tracks, but not erase them; that out of love

and grief, it takes the shape of our shadows,
crouches by trash cans in the mind's back alleys,
surviving on what we refuse. Look above it, instead,
and say that in time the unreconciled settles into place
like a renegade star in some guiding constellation,

and that our altered courses remain the correct ones.
That's what I tell myself in these northern woods.
I call your abandonment grace and believe in it
even more than you. That I might finally move
through this meanwhile and find a place to live.

Instinct

Winter was running out before I was ready—
gray clouds scudding flat-bottomed above
the cornfields and small huddles of houses,
the cold low-roofed light breaking open.
There wasn't any work. I took longer walks.
One day I boarded a bus and stepped off here
with two suitcases and my last twenty.

I found a room in this house, three floors
of women keeping out of each other's way.
Lucille, the rickety shadow above me,
has rented her attic room for life.
She scrubs our kitchen sink every morning,
a ritual with rubber gloves and cleanser,
and water boiled in white enamel bowls.

A cellist has moved into the room below me.
She practices at odd hours, scraping
bow against strings, irregular, urgent—
rasping pitches of some mental schism.
It's a quiet house except for her, except
for the undertones of pipes, doors closing,
phones ringing in rooms with no one home.

I hung a bird feeder from the fire escape
outside my window, but they haven't discovered it.
It's not a place birds would think to land.
I watch that little house swinging in gusts
of north wind against a backdrop of brick.
I'm considering South Dakota, Alberta.
Everywhere you move people ask you why.

As far as I know this is part of the story,
these slight intersections of contiguous lives.
The cellist's song rises like the undersides

78

of memory, the migratory calls of something winged
and flightless. Lucille hangs a sign on the basement doorknob
whenever she descends with trash or laundry,
Dont lock this door I am down there.

Angel Photograph and Dog

In September I drove back to the Midwest—
eleven hundred miles of white, lost weather,
the same people at each turnpike restaurant.
When I reached the northern coast of Michigan
autumn was already underway,
the first leaves falling on my cabin roof,
the furnace broken. I let it go for days,
took long walks around the lake, the mountains
I'd left behind appearing, disappearing.
Sent out handfuls of cheap postcards saying
I am here—water and washed-out sunsets,
photographs of places I hadn't seen.

What is missed is sometimes slow to develop.
I've been thinking of a photograph I saw
before I left. In it, a man my age—
a friend, although our paths have rarely crossed—
was dressed in angel armor and wings,
a backstage picture, black and white,
taken in a tent in eastern Europe.
He'd returned to New Hampshire the day before I left.
We walked to the green, sat at the shade's edge
in the clear, fine-grained heat of noon,
falling back into our intermittent
conversation, its warm pull, opposite, parallel.
And a white and silver dog with sharp black markings
and blue-frost eyes circled us, then curled
to rest behind my friend, curled right up
against his spine, and stayed until we left.
The dog's sleep edged our easy silences—
he seemed to take the shape of something
we were trying to say. About our work,
our restless trust in moving. I don't
remember words as much as tone of voice,
the warm, resilient grass our fingers pulled

and knotted as we spoke. The sun moving on,
hauling its long shadow behind it.

Before we left he took out photographs
from his travels with a theater troupe in Europe,
the stories he'd been telling that afternoon.
He'd kept the pictures until last, he'd said,
to force himself to put them into words.
The angel, smiling, guardian, among them,
a photograph of something invisible.
There are times now in this place it seems important
to have that picture with me—I think of it
as something missing from my life. But then
I think the gift is having seen it only once.
How, missing, missed, it takes this shape.

Notes

"Sherwood Anderson Walks Out" is based on accounts of this episode related in Anderson's *Memoirs* and *A Story Teller's Story*, and in *The Road to Winesburg* by William A. Sutton. The quote at the close of the poem is excerpted from a 1929 letter to Baronness Marie Koskull, included in *Sherwood Anderson: Selected Letters*, edited by Charles E. Modlin.

Part 2 of "Self-Defense" is taken from Starkweather's manuscript, and the italicized portion of part 4 is from a letter to his father. The poem draws on information from magazine articles at the time of the killings, and from James Reinhardt's *The Murderous Trail of Charles Starkweather*, William Allen's *Starkweather*, and *Caril* by Ninette Beaver, B. K. Ripley, and Patricia Trese. The poem also owes a debt to Terence Malick's film, *Badlands*.

About the Author

DEBRA ALLBERY was born in Lancaster, Ohio, in 1957. She studied at Denison University and the College of Wooster (Ohio), where she earned a B.A. in English, and at the University of Iowa, where she received an M.F.A. in Creative Writing. She has been writer-in-residence at Interlochen Arts Academy and Phillips Exeter Academy. Among her awards are a 1986 National Endowment for the Arts Poetry Fellowship and two grants from the New Hampshire State Council on the Arts. She was a winner of the 1989 Discovery Prize of *The Nation*. *Walking Distance* was selected by Ed Ochester from more than eight hundred manuscripts submitted to the 1990 Agnes Lynch Starrett Poetry Prize. Allbery is currently in the graduate English program at the University of Virginia.

Pitt Poetry Series

Ed Ochester, General Editor

Claribel Alegría, *Flowers from the Volcano*
Claribel Alegría, *Woman of the River*
Debra Allbery, *Walking Distance*
Maggie Anderson, *Cold Comfort*
Robin Becker, *Giacometti's Dog*
Michael Benedikt, *The Badminton at Great Barrington; Or, Gustave Mahler
    & the Chattanooga Choo-Choo*
Michael Burkard, *Ruby for Grief*
Siv Cedering, *Letters from the Floating World*
Lorna Dee Cervantes, *Emplumada*
Robert Coles, *A Festering Sweetness: Poems of American People*
Nancy Vieira Couto, *The Face in the Water*
Kate Daniels, *The Niobe Poems*
Kate Daniels, *The White Wave*
Toi Derricotte, *Captivity*
Sharon Doubiago, *South America Mi Hija*
Norman Dubie, *Alehouse Sonnets*
Stuart Dybek, *Brass Knuckles*
Odysseus Elytis, *The Axion Esti*
Jane Flanders, *Timepiece*
Gary Gildner, *Blue Like the Heavens: New & Selected Poems*
Barbara Helfgott Hyett, *In Evidence: Poems of the Liberation of Nazi
    Concentration Camps*
David Huddle, *Paper Boy*
Phyllis Janowitz, *Temporary Dwellings*
Lawrence Joseph, *Curriculum Vitae*
Lawrence Joseph, *Shouting at No One*
Etheridge Knight, *The Essential Etheridge Knight*
Bill Knott, *Poems: 1963–1988*
Ted Kooser, *One World at a Time*
Ted Kooser, *Sure Signs: New and Selected Poems*
Larry Levis, *The Widening Spell of the Leaves*
Larry Levis, *Winter Stars*
Larry Levis, *Wrecking Crew*
Robert Louthan, *Living in Code*
Irene McKinney, *Six O'Clock Mine Report*
Archibald MacLeish, *The Great American Fourth of July Parade*
Peter Meinke, *Liquid Paper: New and Selected Poems*
Peter Meinke, *Night Watch on the Chesapeake*